Native Values
Living in Harmony

Native Values: Living in Harmony

Designed in the USA.
Printed in Canada.

Sealaska Heritage Institute
105 S. Seward St. Suite 201
Juneau, Alaska 99801
907.463.4844

www.sealaskaheritage.org

ISBN: 978-1-946019-11-0

5 4 3 2

Edited by Hannah Lindoff.
Design by Nobu Koch.

Sealaska Heritage Institute photos by Brian Wallace, Nobu Koch, Kathy Dye,
Bill Hess, Jasmine James, and Shgen George.
Page 4-5, courtesy of Nobu Koch.
Page 18-19, courtesy of Sealaska, photo by Daniel Cima.

This book was made possible through funds from the US Department of Education Alaska Native Education Program Grant PR# S356A140060 *Raven Reading: A Culturally Responsive Kindergarten Readiness Program* and PR# S356A170019 *Raven Reads in Southeast Alaska: A Culturally Responsive Kindergarten Readiness Program*. The contents of this book do not necessarily represent the policy of the DOE, and you should not assume endorsement by the Federal Government.

Baby Raven Reads is an award-winning Sealaska Heritage education program promoting a love of learning through culture and community.

Native Values
Living in Harmony

By Rosita Kaahání Worl, Ph.D.

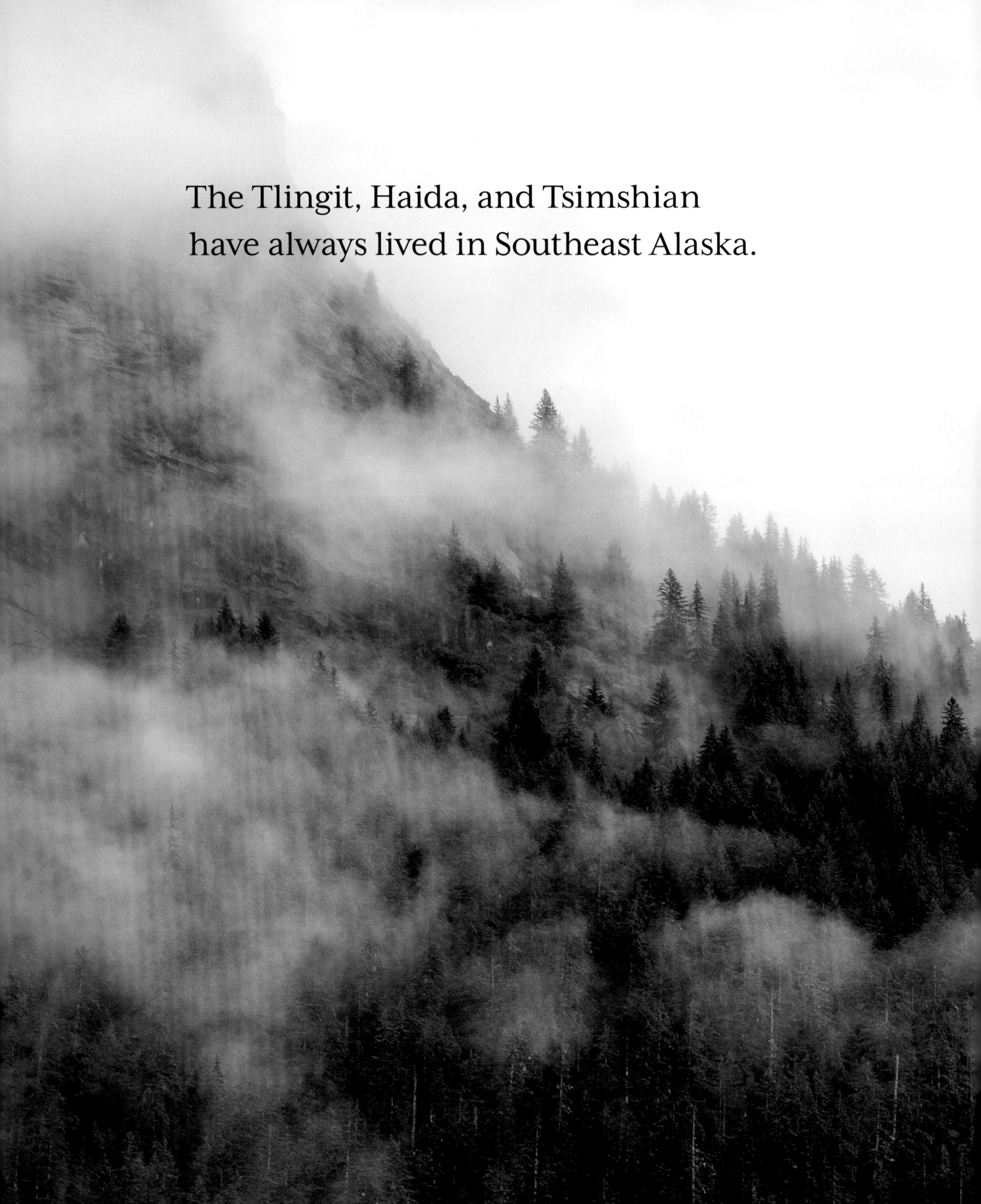

The Tlingit, Haida, and Tsimshian have always lived in Southeast Alaska.

Here, we live off the richness of the land ...

... and sea.

We have large families called *clans*.

We have ceremonies and bring out our precious clan treasures.

We have beliefs called *values*.
Our values make our culture
and our peoples strong.

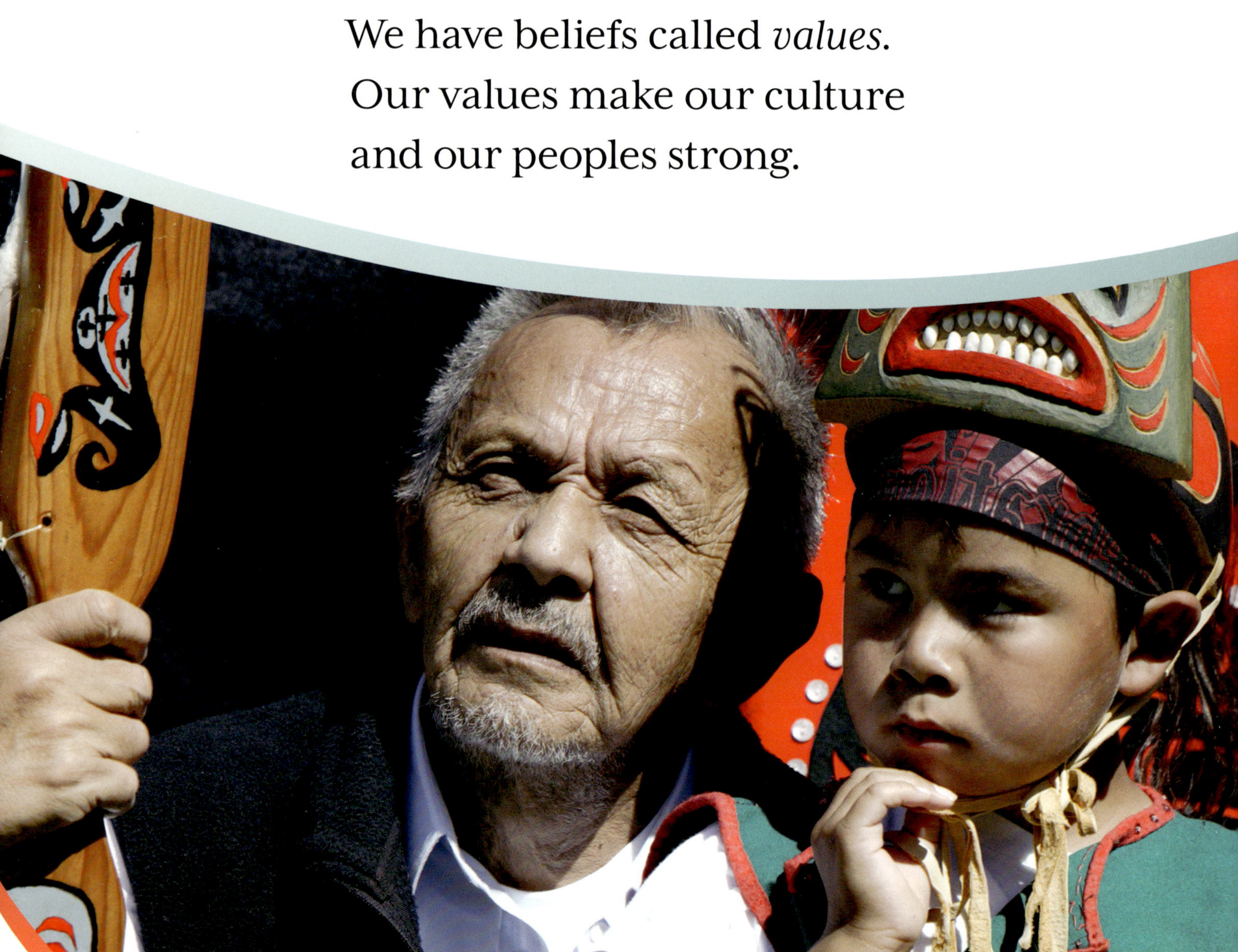

Four major values identify us as Native peoples and guide our lives.

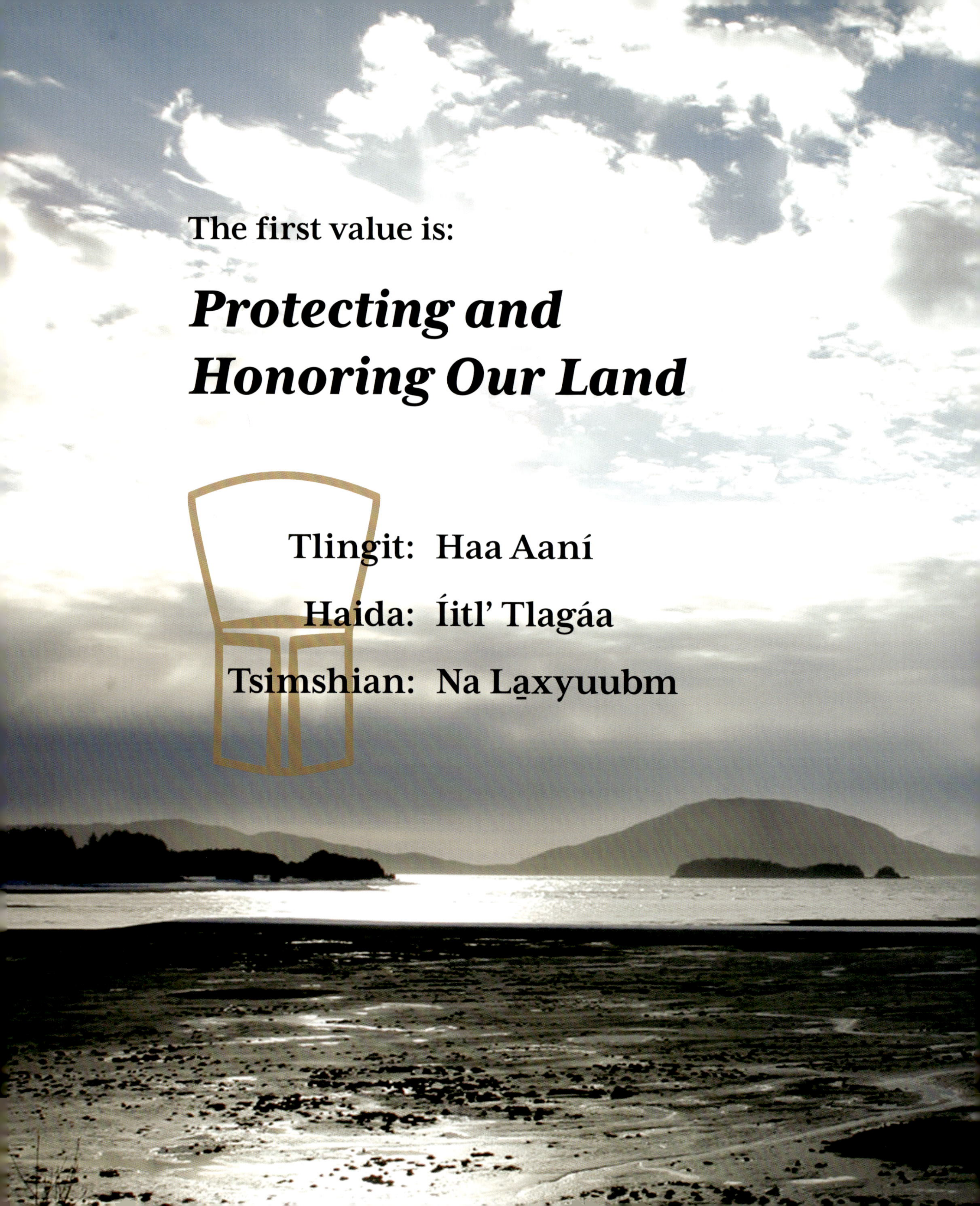

The first value is:

Protecting and Honoring Our Land

Tlingit: Haa Aaní

Haida: Íitl' Tlagáa

Tsimshian: Na La̱xyuubm

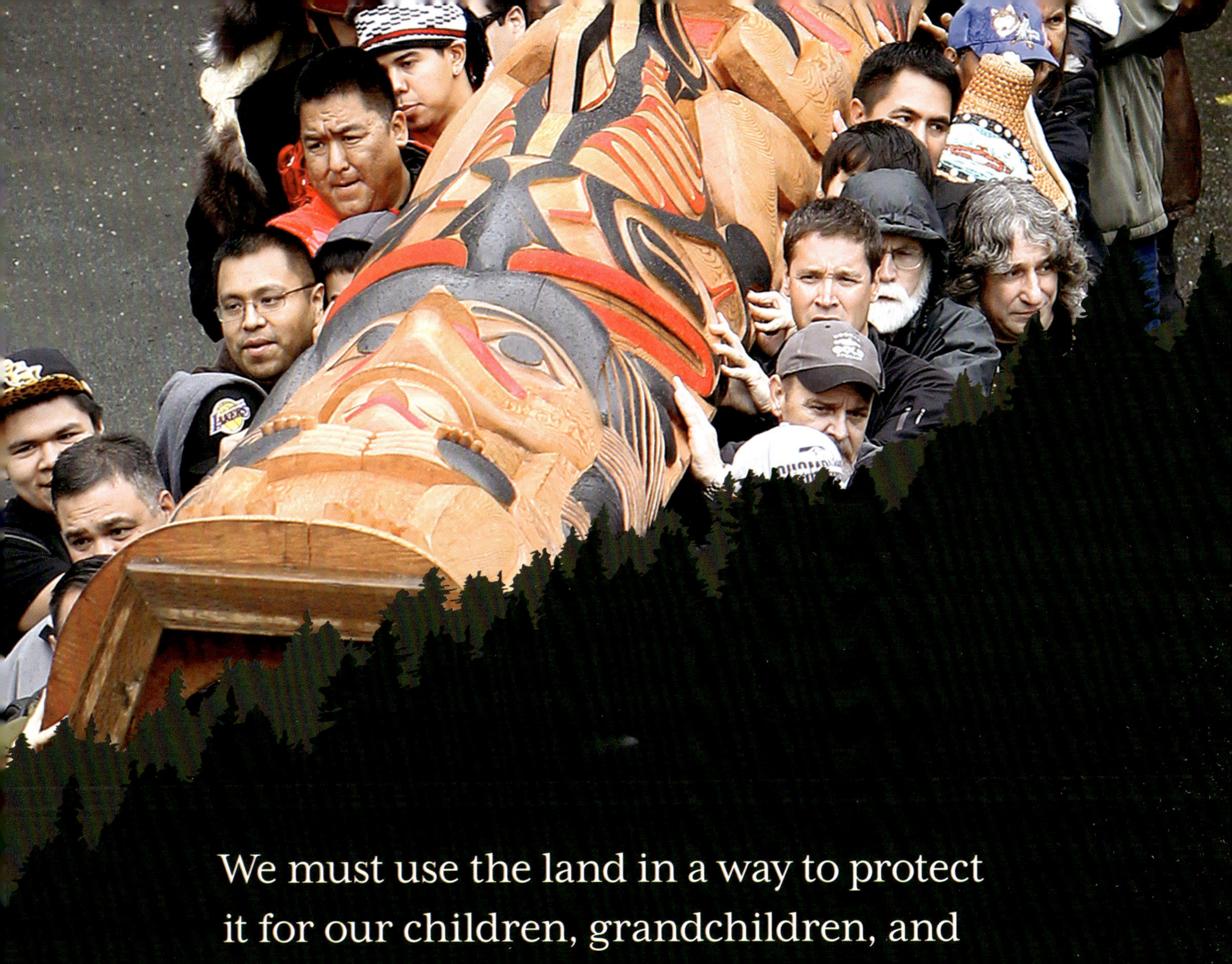

We must use the land in a way to protect it for our children, grandchildren, and those who are yet to be born.

We believe that everything has a spirit, even animals and trees. We use spruce and cedar trees to build large tribal houses, canoes, and totem poles.

We thank the spirits for letting us use the land and its resources.

What are you thankful for today?

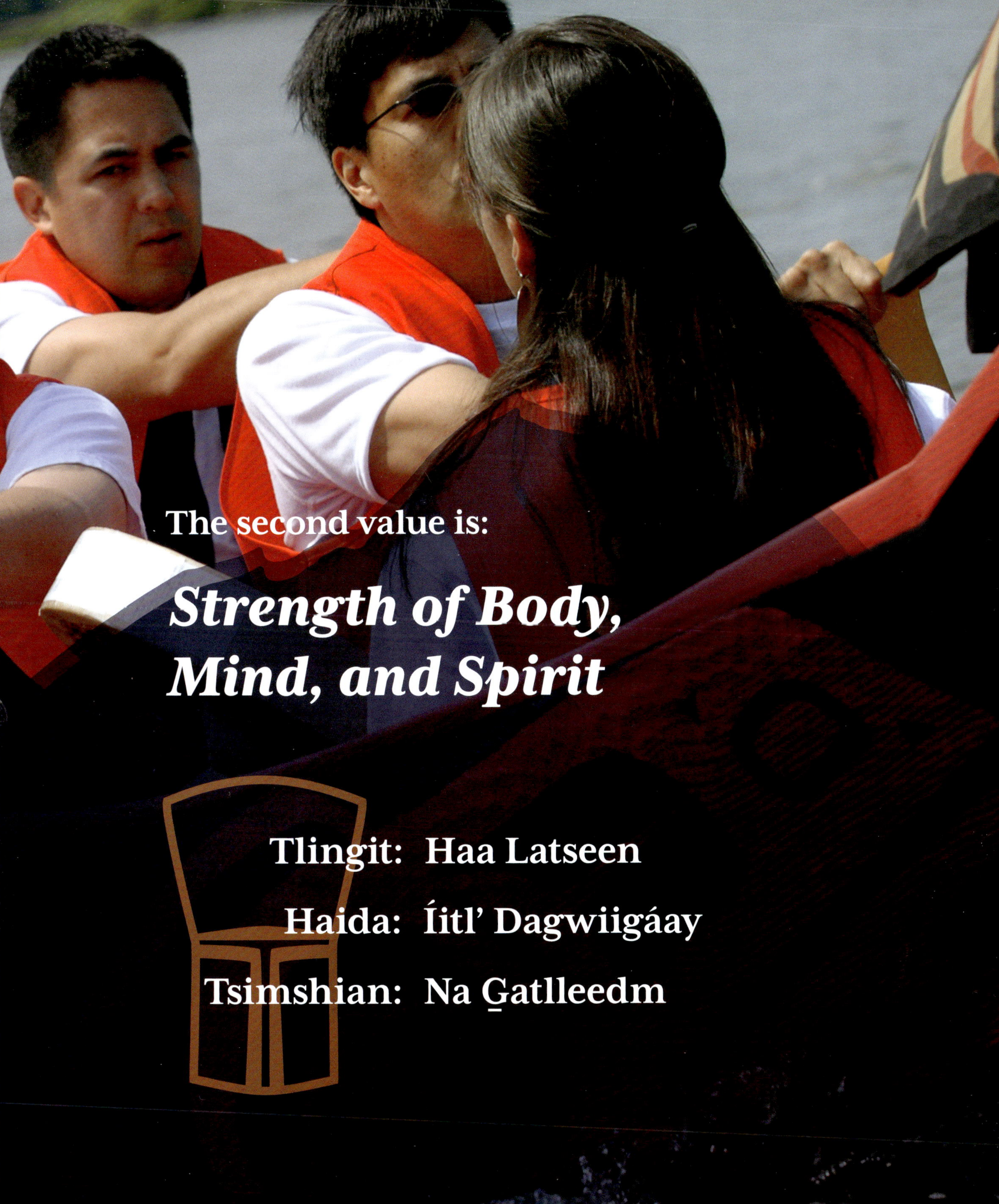

The second value is:

Strength of Body, Mind, and Spirit

Tlingit: Haa Latseen

Haida: Íitl' Dagwiigáay

Tsimshian: Na G̱atlleedm

We must live our lives in a way to be healthy and strong. Salmon, herring, halibut, shellfish, deer, and other food from the land and sea keep our bodies in good health.

We must also have inner strength and speak the truth. We must strengthen our minds, seek knowledge, and do well in life.

We must take care of our families and clan. We share our Native foods so we all may be strong.

What makes you strong?

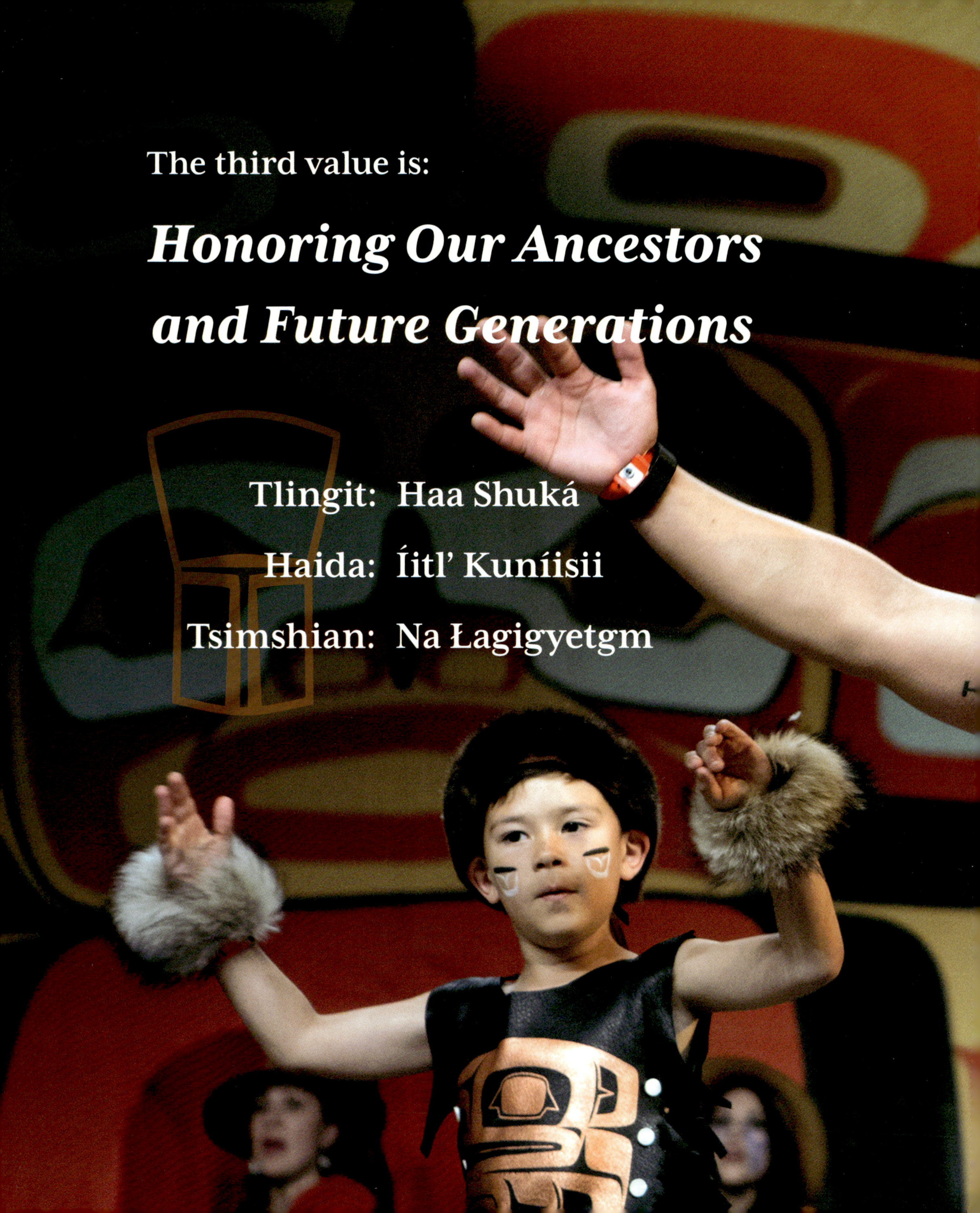

The third value is:

Honoring Our Ancestors and Future Generations

Tlingit: Haa Shuká

Haida: Íitl' Kuníisii

Tsimshian: Na Łagigyetgm

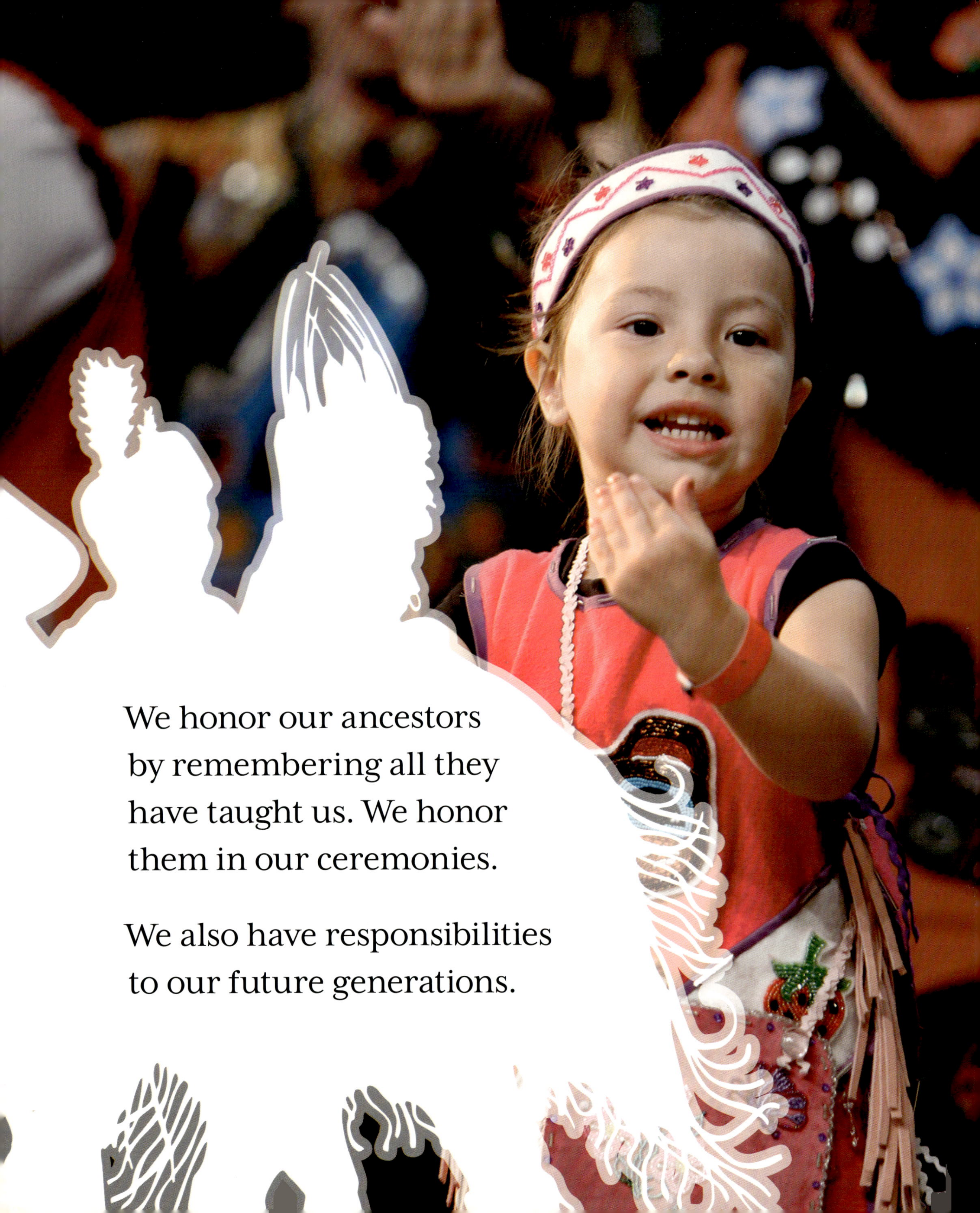

We honor our ancestors by remembering all they have taught us. We honor them in our ceremonies.

We also have responsibilities to our future generations.

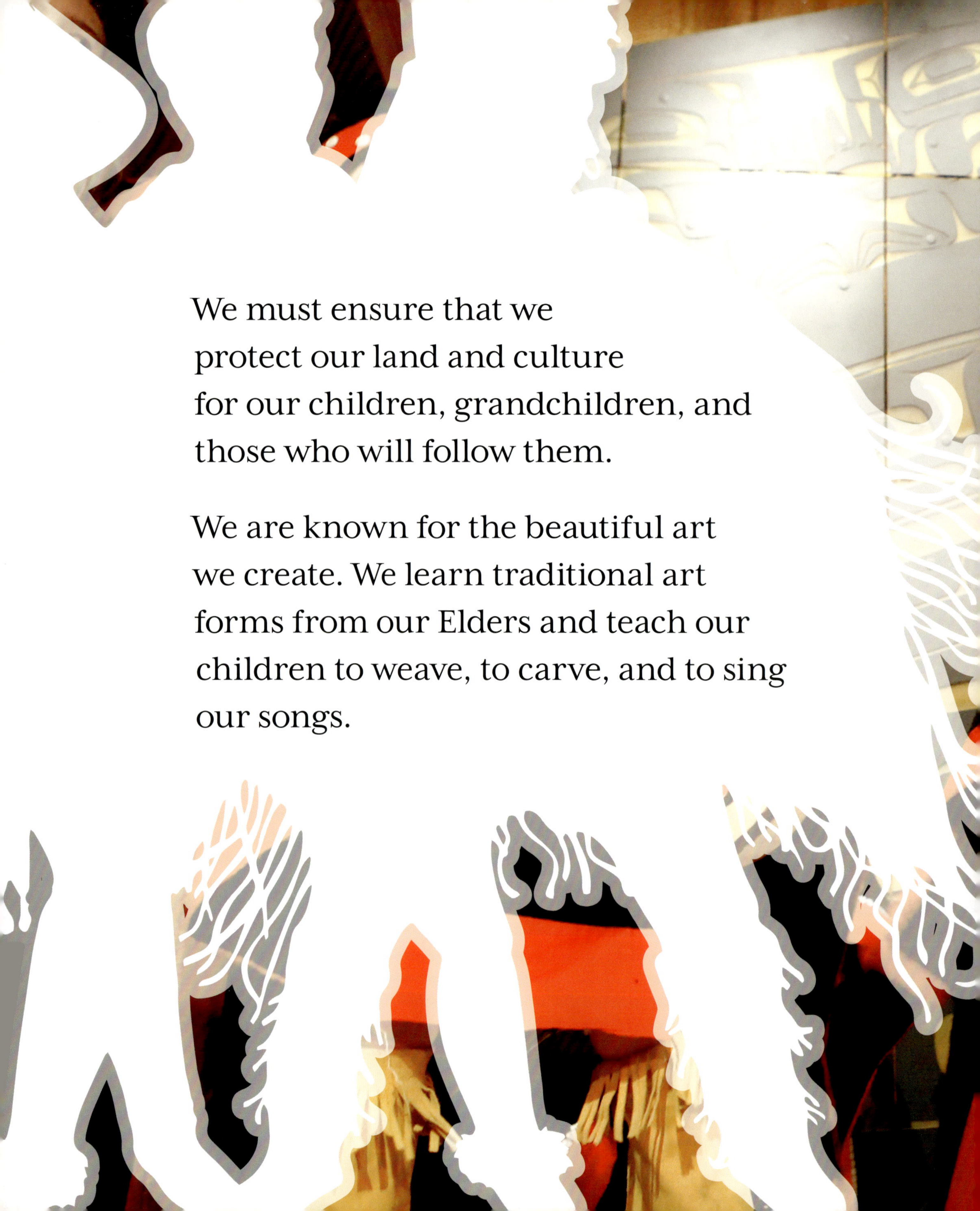

We must ensure that we protect our land and culture for our children, grandchildren, and those who will follow them.

We are known for the beautiful art we create. We learn traditional art forms from our Elders and teach our children to weave, to carve, and to sing our songs.

Do you know a song?

The fourth value is:

Maintaining Social and Spiritual Balance

Tlingit: Wooch Yáx̲

Haida: Gu dlúu

Tsimshian: Ama Mackshm

This value means
we must always live in harmony
with our family and friends.

We must be honest. We must act in ways
to respect our clan members and those
who belong to other clans.

We must respect all other people.
We must respect ourselves.

Close your eyes. You are precious.
We have respect and love for you.

Protecting and Honoring Our Land

Tlingit: Haa Aaní
Haida: Íitl' Tlagáa
Tsimshian: Na La̱xyuubm

Strength of Body, Mind, and Spirit

Tlingit: Haa Latseen
Haida: Íitl' Dagwiigáay
Tsimshian: Na G̱atlleedm

Honoring Our Ancestors and Future Generations

Tlingit: Haa Shuká
Haida: Íitl' Kuníisii
Tsimshian: Na Łagigyetgm

Maintaining Social and Spiritual Balance

Tlingit: Wooch Yáx̲

Haida: Gu dlúu

Tsimshian: Ama Mackshm

about Sealaska Heritage Institute

Sealaska Heritage Institute is a regional Native nonprofit 501(c)(3) corporation. Our mission is to perpetuate and enhance Tlingit, Haida, and Tsimshian cultures. Our goal is to promote cultural diversity and cross-cultural understanding.

Sealaska Heritage was founded in 1980 by Sealaska after being conceived by clan leaders, traditional scholars, and Elders at the first Sealaska Elders Conference. During that meeting, the Elders likened Native culture to a blanket. They told the new leaders that their hands were growing weary of holding onto the metaphorical blanket, this "container of wisdom." They said they were transferring this responsibility to Sealaska, the regional Native corporation serving Southeast Alaska. In response, Sealaska founded Sealaska Heritage to operate cultural and educational programs.

about Baby Raven Reads

Sealaska Heritage sponsors *Baby Raven Reads*, a program that promotes a love of learning through culture and community. The program is for families with Alaska Native children up to age 5. Among other things, events include family nights at the Walter Soboleff Building clan house, Shuká Hít, where families are invited to join us for storytelling, songs, and other cultural activities. Participants also receive free books through the program.

Baby Raven Reads was made possible through funds from the US Department of Education Alaska Native Education Program Grant PR# S356A140060 *Raven Reading: A Culturally Responsive Kindergarten Readiness Program* running from 2015-2017.